Would You Rather?

Animals

EDITION

Would You Rather?

Animals

EDITION

Answer Wild and Wacky Questions to Win a Roaring Good Game

LINDSEY DALY

Z KIDS • NEW YORK

Published in the United States by Z Kids, an imprint of
Zeitgeist™, a division of Penguin Random House LLC, New York.
zeitgeistpublishing.com

Zeitgeist™ is a trademark of Penguin Random House LLC
ISBN: 9780593886335
Ebook ISBN: 9780593886229

Cover art © by ONYXprj/Getty Images
Interior art © by Arthur Balitskii/Shutterstock.com, mhatzapa/Shutterstock.com, Victoria Sergeeva/Shutterstock.com, Vector Tradition/Shutterstock.com, SofiaV/Shutterstock.com, In Art/Shutterstock.com, Valentina I/Shutterstock.com, putra-purwanto/Getty Images, Vect0r0vich/Getty Images, eugeneharnam/Getty Images, PandaVector/Getty Images, Darja Kuznetsova/Getty Images, Olena Zhuravska/Getty Images

Cover design by Katy Brown
Interior design by Erin Yeung
Author photograph © by Jocelyn Morales

Printed in the United States of America
1st Printing

For Christian. Life is better with you.

Special thanks to Jake Dicob
for his creative contributions.

Contents

Introduction

Everyone in the world has their own interests and hobbies, but one thing most people share is a love and fascination for animals. *Would You Rather? Animals Edition* offers more than 160 questions about the fascinating creatures who share Earth with us. What better way to pass time in restaurants or on road trips than by discussing feathered friends and creepy crawlers?

This set of "Would You Rather?" questions are an excellent way to learn more about animals and are designed to start funny, thoughtful, and creative discussions. The questions are for kids ages 8–12, but they're sure to entertain the whole family. You never know what fascinating details you might learn about what and *how* other people think!

Would You Rather? Animals Edition is designed to be played as a game, with winners for individual questions and chapters, and points based on humor, logic, and overall creativity. In this book, you'll find funny and thought-provoking scenarios revolving around our furry (and non-furry) friends that will stretch your imagination and put your mind to the test. Get ready to show off your critical-thinking skills: have fun and go "wild" for the questions in these pages!

Rules of the Game

Get a group of friends or family members together for a game of wits and creativity. The more the better!

* The game is played in eight rounds, with twenty questions in each round.
* Players rotate the responsibility of being the "judge" and read the question aloud to the group.
* Players will then respond with an explanation and take turns sharing their answers.
* The judge of that round will choose the best answer based on humor, creativity, or logic. Write the winner's name in the space provided below the question and assign them one point. If only two people are playing, the judge (the player reading the question) assigns 1 to 5 points for the answer

(5 being the best answer) and records it with the other player's name in the space provided below the question.

* When all players complete the round, tally up the points to determine the winner for that round.
* In the event of a tie at the end of a round, the players who are tied will answer the tiebreaker question. All remaining players will vote on the best answer. If only two people are playing, whoever makes the other player laugh wins.
* When all players complete the book, the winner of the most rounds is the champion!

ROUND 1

Perfect Pets

Would you rather

have a snake loose in your house

or

a rat?

WINNER: POINTS:

Would you rather

eat wet dog food

or

hamster pellets?

WINNER: POINTS:

Would you rather
design your own line of cat toys
or
dog clothes?

WINNER: POINTS:

Would you rather
spend a week living in a human-size hamster cage
or
a horse stable?

WINNER: POINTS:

Would you rather

take a bath with 100 goldfish

or

sleep in a bed with 20 gerbils?

WINNER: POINTS:

Would you rather

ride a vision-impaired horse

or

walk 10 dogs at the same time?

WINNER: POINTS:

Would you rather
be in a room for an hour
with 50 puppies
or
kittens?

WINNER: POINTS:

Would you rather
have a parrot that constantly
mimicked you
or
screamed once an hour?

WINNER: POINTS:

Would you rather

have the fluffiest pet on earth

or

the friendliest?

WINNER: POINTS:

Would you rather

smell like a guinea pig

or

have dog breath?

WINNER: POINTS:

Would you rather
be able to fly like a bird
or
breathe underwater like a fish?

WINNER: POINTS:

Would you rather
have sharp claws
like a cat
or
a heightened sense
of smell like a dog?

WINNER: POINTS:

Would you rather

have a pet boa constrictor

or

a tarantula?

WINNER: POINTS:

Would you rather

transform into a turtle for a day

or

a hermit crab?

WINNER: POINTS:

Would you rather
have an aquarium full
of tropical fish
or
an aviary filled with birds?

WINNER: POINTS:

Would you rather
go to the bathroom in a litter box
or
outside in a public area?

WINNER: POINTS:

Would you rather

have a bird beak

or

bunny ears?

WINNER: POINTS:

Would you rather

sleep in a doghouse

or

a cat condo?

WINNER: POINTS:

Would you rather
have the body of a snake
or
a ferret?

WINNER: POINTS:

Would you rather
have your laugh be replaced
with a meow
or
a bark?

WINNER: POINTS:

TIEBREAKER

Would you rather

shed your skin like a snake

or

have the short memory span of a goldfish?

WINNER: POINTS:

WINNER: ________________________

TOTAL POINTS: ________________________

ROUND 2

Backyard Bugs and Beyond

Would you rather
have your house infested
with termites
or
cockroaches?

WINNER: POINTS:

Would you rather
be covered in 100 of
the same insects
or
a variety?

WINNER: POINTS:

Would you rather
have eight legs
or
eight eyes?

WINNER: POINTS:

Would you rather
be small enough to
crawl into an anthill
or
fly into a beehive?

WINNER: POINTS:

Would you rather
have the wings of a butterfly
or
a butt that lights up like a firefly?

WINNER: POINTS:

Would you rather
find an ant in your bed
or
a spider?

WINNER: POINTS:

Would you rather
walk through a field of ticks
or
wasps?

WINNER: POINTS:

Would you rather
eat a chocolate-covered beetle
or
cicada?

WINNER: POINTS:

Would you rather
be covered in polka dots
like a ladybug
or
stripes like a hornet?

WINNER: POINTS:

Would you rather
be a beekeeper
or
study bees?

WINNER: POINTS:

Would you rather

have a caterpillar crawl
up your nose

or

into your ear?

WINNER: POINTS:

Would you rather

have the quick reflexes
of a fly

or

be able to spin a web
like a spider?

WINNER: POINTS:

Would you rather

discover a human-size grasshopper
in your backyard

or

centipede?

WINNER: POINTS:

Would you rather

be attacked by a swarm of moths

or

ladybugs?

WINNER: POINTS:

Would you rather
spend a day as a worm
or
a praying mantis?

WINNER: POINTS:

Would you rather
have an exoskeleton
or
wings?

WINNER: POINTS:

Would you rather
discover spider eggs inside the food you just ate
or
maggots?

WINNER: POINTS:

Would you rather
have skin that is fuzzy
or
slimy?

WINNER: POINTS:

Would you rather

have bedbugs

or

fleas?

WINNER: POINTS:

Would you rather

have a pet cockroach

or

spotted lantern fly?

WINNER: POINTS:

TIEBREAKER

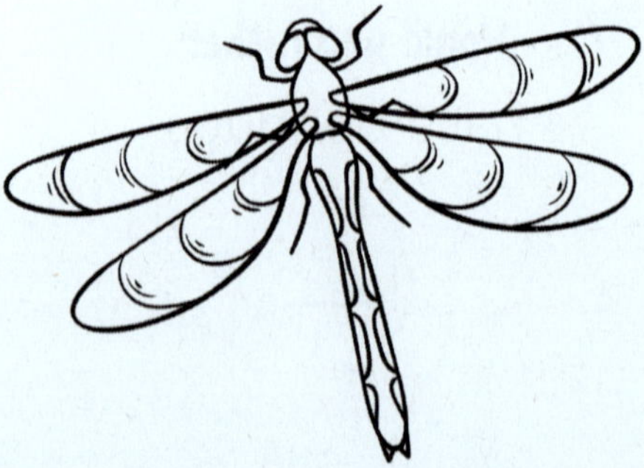

Would you rather

ride on the back of a giant dragonfly

or

bumblebee?

WINNER: POINTS:

WINNER: ______________________________

TOTAL POINTS: ______________________________

ROUND 3

Underwater Creatures

Would you rather
swim with sharks
or
dolphins?

WINNER: POINTS:

Would you rather
get stung by a jellyfish
or
pinched by a crab?

WINNER: POINTS:

Would you rather

breathe through a blowhole

or

gills?

WINNER: POINTS:

Would you rather

have giant walrus tusks

or

sea lion whiskers?

WINNER: POINTS:

Would you rather
drink clam juice
or
squid ink?

WINNER: POINTS:

Would you rather
live inside a protective shell like a crab
or
have rows of sharp teeth like a shark?

WINNER: POINTS:

Would you rather

have a pet otter

or

seal?

WINNER: POINTS:

Would you rather

be the size of a whale

or

a shrimp?

WINNER: POINTS:

Would you rather
be a marine mammal
or
a crustacean?

WINNER: POINTS:

Would you rather
go scuba diving to look
at sea creatures
or
take a tour in a submarine?

WINNER: POINTS:

Would you rather
ride on the back of a dolphin
or
a sea turtle?

WINNER: POINTS:

Would you rather
have lobster claws as hands
or
octopus arms?

WINNER: POINTS:

Would you rather
get a sea urchin stuck in
your bathing suit
or
an electric eel?

WINNER: POINTS:

Would you rather
go snorkeling in the
Great Barrier Reef
or
train dolphins at an
aquarium?

WINNER: POINTS:

Would you rather

read the minds of sea creatures

or

have them understand you?

WINNER: POINTS:

Would you rather

help baby sea turtles find their way into the ocean safely

or

work with injured dolphins?

WINNER: POINTS:

Would you rather
swim in a pool with a
giant manta ray
or
a hammerhead shark?

WINNER: POINTS:

Would you rather
drink a glass of salt water
or
eat seaweed?

WINNER: POINTS:

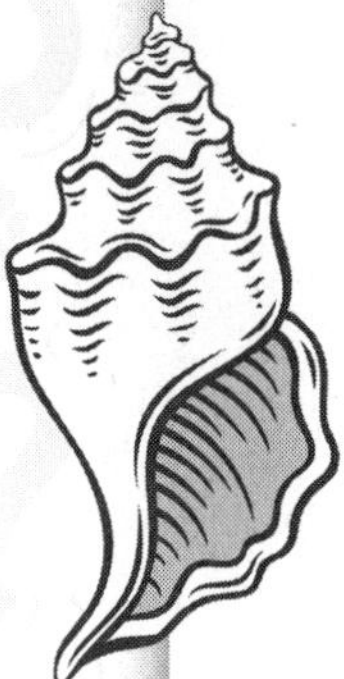

Would you rather

find a starfish on the beach

or

a conch shell?

WINNER: POINTS:

Would you rather

pet a manatee

or

a walrus?

WINNER: POINTS:

TIEBREAKER

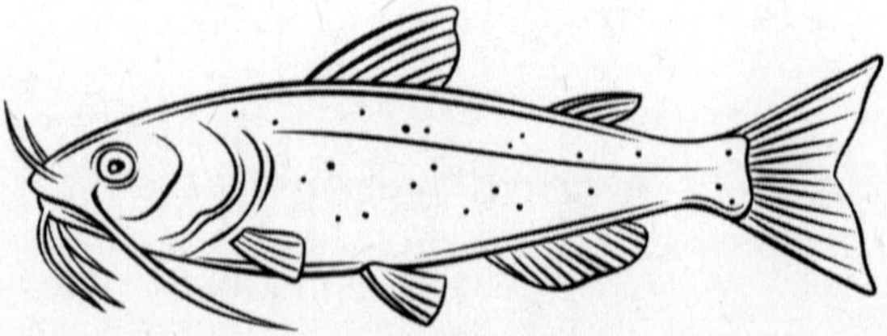

Would you rather

sit in a tank with 50 catfish

or

seahorses?

WINNER: POINTS:

WINNER: ____________________

TOTAL POINTS: ____________________

ROUND

4

Feathered Friends

Would you rather
have eyes on the sides
of your head
or
a neck that can rotate
360 degrees?

WINNER: POINTS:

Would you rather
see a hummingbird in
your backyard
or
a bald eagle?

WINNER: POINTS:

Would you rather
have the voice of a parrot
or
a crow?

WINNER: POINTS:

Would you rather
waddle when you walk
or
always stand on one leg?

WINNER: POINTS:

Would you rather

have webbed feet

or

sharp talons?

WINNER: POINTS:

Would you rather

have a long ostrich neck

or

long flamingo legs?

WINNER: POINTS:

Would you rather

randomly quack
like a duck

or

shriek like a seagull?

WINNER: POINTS:

Would you rather

be a snowbird

or

a tropical bird?

WINNER: POINTS:

Would you rather

have hair the color of

peacock feathers

or

parrot feathers?

WINNER: POINTS:

Would you rather

be woken up by the sound

of a rooster crowing

or

a woodpecker pecking a tree?

WINNER: POINTS:

Would you rather
adopt a baby owl
or
a baby penguin?

WINNER: POINTS:

Would you rather
spend a day bird-watching
or
volunteering at a bird sanctuary?

WINNER: POINTS:

Would you rather
study penguins in Antarctica
or
tropical birds in the rainforest?

WINNER: POINTS:

Would you rather
have a duck bill
or
a pelican beak?

WINNER: POINTS:

Would you rather

be as small as a hummingbird

or

as big as an ostrich?

WINNER: POINTS:

Would you rather

be able to imitate a mockingbird

or

have waterproof feathers
like a duck?

WINNER: POINTS:

Would you rather
sleep in a nest in a tree
or
in a hole in the ground?

WINNER: POINTS:

Would you rather
get pooped on by a seagull
or
pecked at by a crow?

WINNER: POINTS:

Would you rather
be turned into a pigeon
or
a chicken?

WINNER: POINTS:

Would you rather
ride on the back
of an emu
or
a pelican?

WINNER: POINTS:

TIEBREAKER

Would you rather

be graceful like a swan

or

fierce like an eagle?

WINNER: POINTS:

WINNER: ______________________________

TOTAL POINTS: ______________________________

ROUND

5

Reptiles, Amphibians, and More!

Would you rather
lick a slimy toad
or
a scaly iguana?

WINNER: POINTS:

Would you rather
have a split tongue like a lizard
or
a long tail?

WINNER: POINTS:

Would you rather

be trapped in a room
with a crocodile

or

a python?

WINNER: POINTS:

Would you rather

blend in with your surroundings
like a chameleon

or

have the strength of a
boa constrictor?

WINNER: POINTS:

Would you rather

turn into a giant Komodo dragon
for a day

or

a tiny salamander?

WINNER: POINTS:

Would you rather

move as slow as a tortoise

or

have no legs like a snake?

WINNER: POINTS:

Would you rather
eat insects
or
mice?

WINNER: POINTS:

Would you rather
live in a swamp
or
a desert?

WINNER: POINTS:

Would you rather
be chased by an alligator
or
a snake?

WINNER: POINTS:

Would you rather
find a snapping turtle
in your bedroom
or
a cobra?

WINNER: POINTS:

Would you rather

be immune to snake venom

or

all poisonous plants?

WINNER: POINTS:

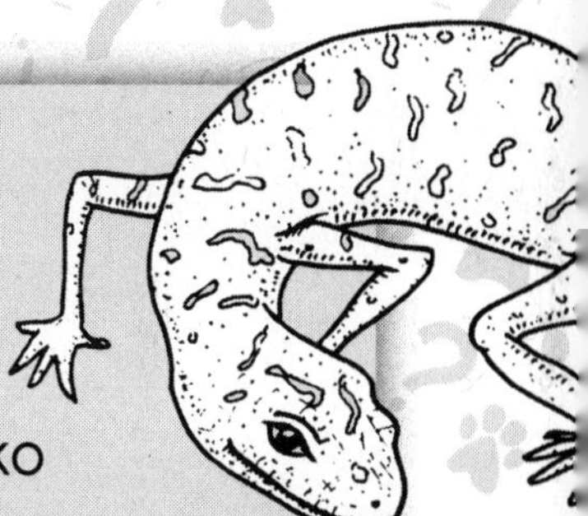

Would you rather

have a pet gecko

or

axolotl?

WINNER: POINTS:

Would you rather
watch tadpoles turn into frogs
or
snakes hatch from their eggs?

WINNER: POINTS:

Would you rather
have fangs
or
a shell?

WINNER: POINTS:

Would you rather
eat only meat
or
plants?

WINNER: POINTS:

Would you rather
hibernate every winter
or
go through a metamorphosis?

WINNER: POINTS:

Would you rather
live in the woodlands
or
a rainforest?

WINNER: POINTS:

Would you rather
be cold-blooded
or
nocturnal?

WINNER: POINTS:

Would you rather

have a heightened sense of smell like a snake

or

hearing like an alligator?

WINNER: POINTS:

Would you rather

be able to breathe through your skin

or

hold your breath for an extended period?

WINNER: POINTS:

TIEBREAKER

Would you rather

have the skin of a crocodile

or

a toad?

WINNER: POINTS:

WINNER: ______________________________

TOTAL POINTS: ______________________________

ROUND 6

Farm Animals

Would you rather

smell like horse manure

or

spoiled milk?

WINNER: POINTS:

Would you rather

oink in between every word you spoke

or

moo?

WINNER: POINTS:

Would you rather
clean out horse
stables every day
or
a chicken coop?

WINNER: POINTS:

Would you rather
have horns like a goat
or
a long neck like an alpaca?

WINNER: POINTS:

Would you rather
watch chicks hatch
or
the birth of a calf?

WINNER: POINTS:

Would you rather
grow a layer of sheep's wool
on top of your skin
or
chicken feathers?

WINNER: POINTS:

Would you rather
live with a herd
of alpacas
or
a flock of ostriches?

WINNER: POINTS:

Would you rather
bleat like a goat
or
gobble like a turkey?

WINNER: POINTS:

Would you rather
ride a donkey through the mountains
or
a horse on the beach?

WINNER: POINTS:

Would you rather
carry a pig around with you all day
or
a chicken?

WINNER: POINTS:

Would you rather

have a curly tail like a pig

or

black spots like a cow?

WINNER: POINTS:

Would you rather

try to catch a runaway chicken

or

herd a group of lost sheep?

WINNER: POINTS:

Would you rather
have a cowbell attached
to your neck
or
a saddle on your back?

WINNER: POINTS:

Would you rather
have a goat follow you
everywhere you go
or
an emu?

WINNER: POINTS:

Would you rather
raise a lamb
or
a piglet?

WINNER: POINTS:

Would you rather
drink milk directly from
a cow's udders
or
eat an egg that was
just laid by a hen?

WINNER: POINTS:

Would you rather
have donkey teeth
or
a pig nose?

WINNER: POINTS:

Would you rather
visit a reindeer farm
in Alaska
or
a camel farm
in California?

WINNER: POINTS:

Would you rather

have chicken legs

or

horse hooves?

WINNER: POINTS:

Would you rather

drink water from a trough

or

eat hay?

WINNER: POINTS:

TIEBREAKER

Would you rather

have wattles hanging from your neck like a rooster

or

cow nostrils?

WINNER: POINTS:

WINNER

WINNER: ______________________

TOTAL POINTS: ______________________

ROUND

7

Big Beasts

Would you rather
be able to roar like a lion
or
howl like a wolf?

WINNER: POINTS:

Would you rather
ride a manatee
or
a cheetah?

WINNER: POINTS:

Would you rather
hug a gorilla
or
a grizzly bear?

WINNER: POINTS:

Would you rather
trim a lion's mane
or
wash a shark?

WINNER: POINTS:

Would you rather
reindeer followed you
everywhere
or
pandas?

WINNER: POINTS:

Would you rather
have elephant-size ears
or
a nose shaped like
a rhinoceros horn?

WINNER: POINTS:

Would you rather

ride a camel in the desert

or

an elephant in the forest?

WINNER: POINTS:

Would you rather

be a tour guide on a safari

or

a whale-watching boat?

WINNER: POINTS:

Would you rather
be chased by a moose
or
a bobcat?

WINNER: POINTS:

Would you rather
have the memory of an elephant
or
the strength of a gorilla?

WINNER: POINTS:

Would you rather

work for an organization
that stops poachers

or

saves whales from captivity?

WINNER: POINTS:

Would you rather

have a footrace against a cheetah

or

swim alongside a shark?

WINNER: POINTS:

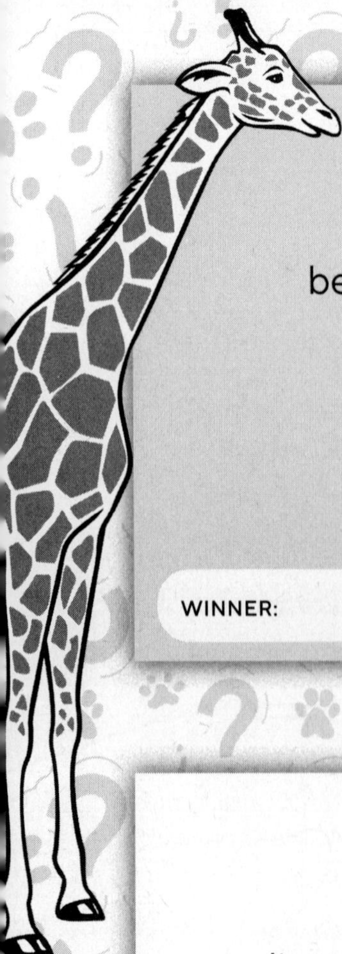

Would you rather
be as tall as a giraffe
or
as wide as a
hippopotamus?

WINNER: POINTS:

Would you rather
live with a pack of wolves
for a month
or
a band of gorillas?

WINNER: POINTS:

Would you rather
cuddle with a family
of polar bears
or
alpacas?

WINNER: POINTS:

Would you rather
have two large humps on your back
or
tusks in your mouth?

WINNER: POINTS:

Would you rather

be covered with spots like a cheetah

or

large wrinkles like an elephant?

WINNER: POINTS:

Would you rather

have a buffalo stuck in your house

or

a capybara?

WINNER: POINTS:

Would you rather
box a kangaroo
or
wrestle an anaconda?

WINNER: POINTS:

Would you rather
store water like a camel
or
repel flies like a zebra?

WINNER: POINTS:

TIEBREAKER

Would you rather

race your best friend
riding on ostriches

or

panthers?

WINNER: POINTS:

WINNER: ______________________________

TOTAL POINTS: ______________________________

ROUND

8

Little Critters

Would you rather

live off bamboo like a red panda

or

eucalyptus like a koala?

WINNER: POINTS:

Would you rather

swing from tree to tree like a monkey

or

glide through the air like a flying squirrel?

WINNER: POINTS:

Would you rather

get a bat caught in your hair

or

bump into a porcupine?

WINNER: POINTS:

Would you rather

be a meerkat for a day

or

a groundhog?

WINNER: POINTS:

Would you rather

have a bushy tail like a squirrel

or

a flat tail like a beaver?

WINNER: POINTS:

Would you rather

move as slowly as a sloth

or

smell like a skunk?

WINNER: POINTS:

Would you rather
be able to burrow deep
into the earth
or
climb trees with ease?

WINNER: POINTS:

Would you rather
live in a bird's nest
or
a rabbit hole?

WINNER: POINTS:

Would you rather
have the cheeks of a
chipmunk forever
or
porcupine quills for six months
each year?

WINNER: POINTS:

Would you rather
have an otter as a pet
or
a mongoose?

WINNER: POINTS:

Would you rather
be able to communicate
with small animals
or
have the power to shrink
down to their size?

WINNER: POINTS:

Would you rather
be hairless like a naked mole rat
or
covered in fluffy, thick fur
like a chinchilla?

WINNER: POINTS:

Would you rather
sleep hanging upside down
or
wedged in a tree?

WINNER: POINTS:

Would you rather
grow fur for warmth
or
camouflage?

WINNER: POINTS:

Would you rather
rescue a monkey
or
a koala?

WINNER: POINTS:

Would you rather
spend a night in a cave
or
the jungle?

WINNER: POINTS:

Would you rather

have a kangaroo pouch

or

long arms that dangle on the ground?

WINNER: POINTS:

Would you rather

have a squirrel in your attic

or

a bat?

WINNER: POINTS:

Would you rather
have short legs
like a weasel
or
black circles around your
eyes like a raccoon?

WINNER: POINTS:

Would you rather
eat only hay
or
wet leaves?

WINNER: POINTS:

TIEBREAKER

Would you rather

train a monkey to do your chores

or

a fox to retrieve any item you want?

WINNER: POINTS:

WINNER: ______________________________

TOTAL POINTS: ______________________________

WINNER

This certificate
is awarded to

____

for wildly witty answers that made everyone laugh like hyenas. Your creativity and knack for logic sealed the deal, making you the winner!

CONGRATULATIONS!

About the Author

Lindsey Daly grew up in Andover, New Jersey, and graduated from Ramapo College. Lindsey is a middle school social studies teacher and the author of the bestselling Would You Rather? series and card deck. She lives in Morristown, New Jersey.

Parents, for more information about Lindsey and her books, follow her online:

@lindseydalybooks

𝕏 @LindseyDaly10

Hi, parents and caregivers,

We hope your child enjoyed *Would You Rather? Animals Edition*. If you have any questions or concerns about this book, or have received a damaged copy, please contact customerservice@penguinrandomhouse.com. We're here and happy to help.

Also, please consider writing a review on your favorite retailer's website to let others know what you and your child thought of the book!

Sincerely,
The Zeitgeist Team